Revoetry:

Poems from an African British Perspective

Its not often we meet
Spirits that frighten the shadow of defeat
With a heart so warm
Creativity is easily, expressively born
Ascente siste Oyin for simply being You
and may this lifetime be rewarded
With all the blessings due

Peace & love
Bro Tom (April 2011)
x

About Revoetry

Revoetry is a selection of short creative writings by Toyin Agbetu that started life October 2002 and was compiled late 2010.

Acknowledgments

To the Creator, the Ancestors and all those that inspire and encouraged me, I love you in this life, the other life, and will continue to do so in the next...

Donations

For ideological reasons it is the policy of the Ligali Organisation to request donations for its works instead of any fixed monetary price. We oppose the forced economic controls imposed on writers, artists and publishers by the capitalisation of cultural media such as literature. It is hoped this publication will be available for loan in libraries and various educational institutions free of charge, and present in African bookshops and markets all over the world for a donation that reflects the appreciation of those supporting our work.

About Ligali

Ligali is a Pan African Human Rights Organisation that challenges the misrepresentation of African people, culture and history in the British media. We produce progressive Africentric media and education programmes that actively work for self determination, socio-political freedom, physical health and spiritual wealth. Ligali works for the socio-political and spiritual empowerment of African people with heritage direct from Africa or indirectly via African diasporic communities, such as those in the Caribbean and South America.

Revoetry

Poems from an African British Perspective

by

Toyin Agbetu

ligali

Revoetry: Poems from an African British Perspective
Published by the Ligali Organisation

If you're reading this book and did not make a donation, then you can make a
contribution to obtain your own copy.

Ligali
PO Box 1257, London, E5 OUD

Email: mail@ligali.org
Web: www.ligali.org
Tel: 020 8986 1984

ISBN   978-0-9543443-7-5

First Edition: February 2011

dedicated to those I call family and friend
thank you for proving
unconditional love
exists.

In service to our family, with the spirit of our Ancestors

Contents

Introduction

Greetings and welcome to some of the random thoughts, ideas and visions that have dwelled inside my mind. Some of the earlier writings represent my naive and politically immaturity at the time whilst others reflect some of the joy and pain of the spiritual and physical encounters from my life's journey so far.

Creative writing has often helped me heal by granting me the freedom to explore, express and even redress situations through which I may have come to harm in or inadvertently caused injury to others. If some of the writings seem incomplete then it is because they are. I may still be reflecting on the experience, learning the lesson. At times I have seen ugliness, at other times I have been part of it, as an artist and an educator, I can only hope that through my naked words, my spirit transcends it.

> "Rhyme is an attempt to reassemble and reaffirm the possibility of paradise. There is a wholeness, a serenity in sounds coupling to form a memory."
>
> Derek Walcott

Yet as with most works of creative expression, whilst many of these words are deeply personal, in seeking to reconstruct the possibility of an ideal, others may contain exaggerated works of fiction. For some it may be tempting to read between the gaps but I suggest not. I'm really not that clever - bluntness having always been one of my middle names. Simply put, *Revoetry* is like a map of both my aspirations and personal development as a writer, an activist, an African.

The original idea as conceived and developed over seven years ago was that it would accumulate into representing a progressive form of the revolutionary spoken word. Sadly I have found that my lyrics, when translated into written text often comes across rather crudely as the words are meant to be spoken out loud with intent, rhythm and passion and in some instances, to an interactive audience.

The contents of this book therefore, represents my attempts to express my spirit using words that convey my dreams, my fears, my hopes, my desires. it's an intimate journey through the insanity of my mind, it's a diary of my spiritual and political journey. I have omitted some entries because they still feel too raw, to painful and private to share, likewise I have included others because they are conducive for me to learn, reflect and ultimately - heal. Whilst I remain mischievously confident, I am still inherently shy, hence many of the words contained within will undoubtedly make me vulnerable, not only to robust critique but perhaps even ridicule or scorn.

My failings form the backdrop for my strengths, my passions, the fuel of my craft, my heart. I invite you to focus on the message, and not the flawed messenger, I ask that you reflect on the content of my art, not just the form, and through these snapshots of rhyme I also hope this collection serves as cultural ammunition for our freedom fighters engaged in the ideological warfare for the minds of African people.

> *"Ògún does not protect the Truth of what we would like*
> *to be, he guards the Truth of what is."*
> Awo Fá' Lokun Fátunmbi

I do not hide or apologise for any overt Pan Africanist musings and signposting to empowering resources. For if my words reflecting the banality of neo-colonial life are to have functional purpose and cultural relevance beyond creative 'entertainment', then they must always be tempered by the necessity to also normalise themes of strife and liberatory fights within the African global struggle to fully realise natural justice and human rights.

> *"Liberty and dignity are not options."*

 Therefore whilst I write much on both the healing and wounding aspects of relationships, as a child of Mama African it is my deliberate intent to communicate and document that Afromantic connection, alongside our collective responsibilities and individual identities. I write to make our dreams a reality, to tell you I know without a doubt that I am not a 'black' or 'urban' man, a 'slave' descendant or from a 'negro' race. I am a confident and sometimes assertive African with both Yoruba and diasporic African British heritage. A child of the Creator, a descendent of strong, proud African people that continue to survive enslavement throughout Maafa, a writer-musician sharing works designed to heal spirit by teaching love and freedom.

One of my role models the Pan Africanist artist-activist Fela Kuti once said 'music is the weapon'. Hopefully my words and the emancipatory rhythms I hope they encapsulate can help be the bullets to reflect this Truth.

May the Ancestors continue to guide and protect us.

Ase.

Toyin Agbetu
The Ligali Organisation
December 2010

Maafa

(... towards Ma'at)

hope....

'it's hopeless' she said
fearing change would never come
not noting revolution had begun
as their pillars toppled
one
by
one

you see her...
usual ray of light in dark
dimmed as
evil showed its heart
and tried to sow
its seeds
of doubt and misery
whilst
clawing her soul
changing her flow
not realising
the sweat of pure water from
her brow
was that same stream of
positivity
assisting evil
drown in
its
own
filthy
pit of
imperialist
wanton
greed filled history
where
wants and xenophobic seeds
breed
labour, democrat, bnp, republican
and of course... conserva..
...thieves

and yet
even as she cried
she tried

you see her true spirit hadn't died
nor lied
unlike he
who when caught denied
his sick, corrupting nature
used words like 'expenses' 'misplaced'
'immigration' and 'race'
as his parliament disgraced
continued to
implode
and the
heart of xenophobic Britain
became exposed
and boom - EXPLODES

and as his sick democracy publicly elected
supported
hate mongers
as his catholism
denied institutional
deviant sexual
child abusism

- hope -

like the ankh
of eternal life
brought forth
a dream
into being
through a righteous fight
where
Ancestors
protected our warrior spirits,
guiding
providing for
our healer, teacher, worker spirits
and as
tyrants and giants
crossed into the realm
where innocence,
Truth dominated the world
until once again order
through Ma'at
from an African perspective

returned us to The Way
elevated
and once again

.

.

respected

'...it was hopeless' she sang
knowing change will overcome
the smile on her lips
revealing the revolution
had already

.

.

begun.

insane

It's ok to be insane
were fear becomes rare
and night dreams
collide with day mares
an existence where
normality is a world you cannot bear
a word you don't hear
a feeling you can't share
too confident
too shy
wanting to hide
but refusing to deny
purpose?
wanting to fly
but still possessing earthy binds
some worthless?

emotionally intoxicated
high on your pride
fear on your side
ego denied
beside
that Ancestral strength
that guides and resides
with Africa
inside
freely
loving me
whispering
"knowledge of self is spiritual wealth"
as wisdom dictates
that voice
that dream
redeems
cleans
and
means...

...it's ok to be insane
I know
for I am
because

we are
while
insanity
reigns.

i was abducted by aliens

I awoke sweating, fighting, scared
see in my dream
i was abducted by aliens from another world
in this other life they took my brother, sister, cousins, friends
and before our eyes they murdered my mother, father for resisting
as they transported us onto their huge space ship
i called to the Creator for a reason why
and as we flew across the dark blue sky
the stars I knew grew far with time
we could not understand their alien tongue
nor comprehend what wrong we had done
why even now did so many of us have to die
why were they so evil?
why? why?
and as our journey came to an end
to an old cruel continent had destiny sent us
and just before I woke I heard an alien say
the good ship jesus is back again.

plantation

You're free to choose they told him.
said the voices wielding power,
and for those seven and half hours,
he daily contributed to,
that power...
as they took, instead of sharing
laughing as he parted with his cash
robbed, with ingenuity,
through the many guises they called tax.

contributing to a nation,
to which he had no relation
no recognition,
yet cultural submission
a pre requisite for his employ?
an assimilation tool to deploy?
deploy?
employ?
a ploy,
to show his birth had worth,
a valued member of society
yet....
not quite like his masters
deity

yet today his eyes opened,
as he realised the truth,
his head, had been dead,
wed and fed, by the money that owned him,
and not... as he thought, he owed.
but now, he had been told
would he be bold, or remain sold
would he stand up,
or shut up,
would he put up,
or sell up
could the price on his freedom,
be paid for by his..
his..
his..
his..
his..

it's difficult isn't it?

for a moment he was alive,
running free to his dreams,
but now, now,
lunch time
is over.

4

4 what do you stand proud bLACK fan?
4rced to 4get your original clan
4cibly branded with his alien name
4ever cursed with that mark of shame?
4feiting our culture
4 4reign tribes?
4saking our spirit
4gotton our pride
4ging and 4ming
4profit
4 gain
4rums
4 in4mally absolving his blame?

4 whom?
4 who?
4 what do you stand?
4who are you the subservient... man?
4giving your massa
4pieces of gold
4 taking, still raping ancestral homes
4 writing a history
4saking our birth
4 4ming a future without us on earth?
4get that!

4get that fake justice
4get that fake equality
4 knowledge of self with purpose intact
4 deeds for the 4orthcoming revolution are required
4when did you last stand proud black fan?
400 years back, when you be AFRICAN.

made in Africa

Made - in – Africa

three little words that
describe our entire world
that describe
inside of we
and external of thee

made - in – Africa

a truth repeatedly denied
by others intent on lies
denying not our soul
but their own
betraying not our humanity
but their illicit network of global thrones...

as...

in seeking
to subjugate
our spirituality
promoting cult religions
birthed from our singularity

as...

in presenting
a false image of intellect and beauty
denying our diverse originality
creating clones of people
zombies of clan banality
leaders with cheap politrickary
doctors promoting pharmaceutical dependency
bankers breeding commercial insanity
ministers of churchs of gross immorality
soldiers who kill for a salary?

a salary??

damn...

made - in - Africa
three little words
that refelect
a progressive
not regressive reality
three little words
that project our healthy sharing
and not sick possessive societies

made in Africa
a universal
irreversible
unmitigated
simple truth
that once realised
will set
us all
free
.

.

.

.

.

.

.

but first we have to believe
just open our eyes and see that...
time is a healer
for those who have been deceived
that's you and that's
me

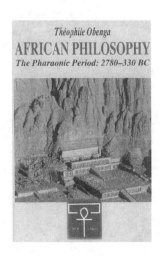

made in Africa
made in Africa
made in Africa

buy one get self free,
but hurry,
stocks won't last..

...we're dying fast.

slave name

As i say my name
i realise i carry the label
of not my story
but his story
his legacy
his brutality
savagery and
in-humanity

they tell me i am free
to be me,
whilst my label does define me
haunts me
brands me
owns me
and ultimately enslaves me

self determination, is the key
"free me"
cries my soul
bold, i do as told
and as the elder does rename
my source of spiritual pain
mama Africa smiles
yes,
another of her womb
is reclaimed.

diaspora

Africans
like trees
growing in a pot
unaware of home
trapped in an alien spot
where our roots are deceived
our leaves culturally diseased
fearful whilst fighting infection against what we are not
branches stretching to reclaim...
all that we forgot.

rant

We're campaigners not complainers
the brown fist means activist
we stand up for justice
with pride in our stride
we never roll over
and play like were dead
nor beg to be fed
when we can work instead

but as we fight for equality
and quality of life
and life free of strife
when afrisms¹ rife
we often get angry
cause we can't turn that cheek
we weren't born to be meek
and we certainly aint weak

we're campaigners not complainers
but were human too
with very short fuses
for language abuses
or cocofied brothas
who shun us for others
and betray our queens
while living the capitalist dream

we're campaigners not complainers
yeah were African too
so what? if were loud when were proud
when were facing a crowd
if you hear what we're saying
if you know what we're saying
if you feel what we're saying
then our job is done.

---

¹ I originally created the word *afrism* to be used as a derivative of racism that was specifically anti-African in character. In reality it felt like a colloquial term for a positive African saying or proverb. Perhaps I should have used 'Afriphobic', anyway I now deliberately use *anti-African* to refer to racism affecting African people.

march

One by one they came
we heard, stomachs turned
passion burned as we learnt
of sorrow, pain... injustice
the crowd grew loud,
passer-by's peeked outside,
as mothers, fathers, siblings
mourned their loss, with tales of violence
and state sanctioned brutality
odes of freedom for
race and economically oppressed minorities

fearing attack, as words hit home
and angry eyes roamed,
the police stayed back,
yet remained,
contained as we were,
they knew, as we knew
this was no
mistake
intellectual debate of....
leaders preaching masterbait

five hundred strong,
we marched that day,
united family and friends,
some still afraid, as others prayed
to downing street,
with banners displayed,
in unison chanting
"what do we want?
justice.
when do we want it?
now."

me3

Me,
i'm proud
a proud African
a proud African fundamentalist
determined and resilient
a persistent pan Africanist
some call me
an extremist
a terrorist
a 'racist'
maybe i'm all three
i'm extreme in my opposition to African inequality
i'm infectious to those who deny African authority
i'm resistant to maafa deniers and their negro puppets
and intellectually i terrorise those that deceive
those who would deny Africans justice
with their inhuman moral hypocrisy.

dreaming revolution

Whenever a person talks to you solely about racism
they divert you from talking of inequality
whenever you are distracted from thinking of equality
you are prevented of dreaming revolution.

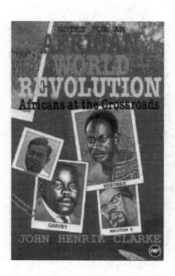

struggle (0, 7, 35, 343, 1492, 1791, 1804, 1884, 1967, 1981, 2007...)

..and this system
that continues to exist
where our people
forced,
persist to resist...

words hurt

Sticks and stones will break your bones
if you use them to oppress me
i will not turn the other cheek
or sing we shall overcome
as you load those literary bullets
into that vile racist vocal gun

sticks and stones will break your bones
if you use your words to disrespect me
if my African identity you cannot respect
and forever in your eyes i'm some kind of suspect
as your laws and justice fails to protect
me
and my community
when instead of African you label me coloured, negro, black
telling me chill bro chill you aint under attack
you've been had
its just political correctness gone mad,
my..... my...
n word
well then my sticks and stones will break your bones
till your words never again - can ever hurt me.

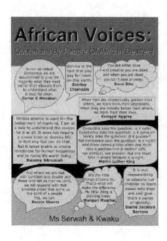

shut the back up

Wherever we go
there's that crowd
in the rear
talking, disrupting as we teach.

society has placed monetary value
on their achievements
validating their existence
thereby in their own mind
eradicating our need for resistance.

yet...
when massa say jump
the back say's "HOW HIGH"
when we say we still enslaved
they
cry in denial

now we know that those people
feel we're talking too loud
"just be cool negroid black,
we aint under attack"
for the back see us as negative
not positive and proud
for when we cry PAN AFRICAN
they scream "racial divide"

and then,
they hide
in the shadows
at the back of that bus,
living luxuries they've earnt
by making no fuss

yet, still we stand
as simple activists,
freeing minds,
whilst the back make jokes
rejecting,
history,
culture,
and identity

for the
millionth time

for
when we say liberation,
they sigh with despair
and
when we mention racism,
they claim "all is now fair"

but the view from the front,
is clear for all to see
those in the rear
may not believe
simply 'cause..
they cannot perceive.
check it out,
we don't deceive.

but the back still attacks
when we stand
shouting loud
but despite this,
despite that,
despite spite,
we still exist.
WE STILL EXIST

..as that social conscience they fear
the ethical nag
that won't sag
just tag
those who lag
and request that you.....
please
please
please
just
shut
the
back
up.

Wounded

(betrayal, loneliness and pain)

betrayal

Nothing hurts like betrayal
physical wounds heal
congeal
blood dries
bones mend
again and
again
but spirit torn
as zombies swarm
vacuous entities
spouting alien ideologies
convinced
of their overseer supremacy
agents of white male supremacy
anti nature degeneracy
in Truth....

...simply masking
their own indolent inadequacies
enslaved to massa
through currency
breeding docility
violent instability
moral impotency
they look at me
they don't see me
don't see we are one
instead go for their guns
conscious African
needs to be made unconscious

its fun!

throwing blows to my head
swearing
wishing me dead
cussing
seeing nothing but red

its fun!

punching me in the stomach

ripping my shirt from my chest
grabbing my bag in jest
it doesn't matter I haven't done anything wrong

its fun!

attack
attack
no longer brother
i am now their other
attack
attack
no longer family
am now the other
attack
attack
now joined by police
hoisted off my feet
cheers as i'm dragged semi naked
into a jubilant crowd
chained once again
recaptured
as house negroes on the float grin
"look massa got toby" again
"that Kunta was never my friend"

I talk
taut
dialogue
with
arresting
force officers
wrought with pain
of
"assault"
to no avail
they cannot act on instinct
they cannot act on Truth
they cannot act beyond that what they see before them..
..an African daring to honour his Ancestors?

the prancing negroes
dance on
the crowds follow
continue the new song

"the audacity"
"...who is he"
"...to tell we"
unknowingly
spectators to the continuing story of their own demise
in a tale where they are the despised
and yet unwittingly
willingly providing the entertainment
they are the entertainment
controlled through
state containment
fate contained
sprit stained
again and again

so chained
and in pain
i walk
surrounded by police
observed by thousands
in a virtual coliseum
all in silence
not one seeks to help
not one seeks to help
no-one seeks to help
no-one
not one
one

its fun!

its carnivorous carnival
"mate - that's what it about"
"celebrate!"
"celebrate what?" I think
but my thoughts are drowned out
as the noise
imposes its will
my gladiator status has been temporarily repealed
my fate by judges for injustice to be once again sealed

meanwhile
the BBC float
1xtra
denotes;

"the African role is to entertain,
that's when we give you fame,
none of this dignified Ancestor game,
leading to blame,
causing massa shame"

so instead
as i'm dragged through the crowd semi naked
men avoiding eye contact
women winking obsessing on my bare chest
"dangerous African" arousing jungle fever
elders look down at me shame faced
"disgrace"

only the young Africans
share my pain with empathy
some not knowing detail
but feeling it the same
and for minutes I walk
bare-chested
but proud
through that crowd
flanked by massa soldiers
chains behind my back
spirit still intact
despite
fact
leaving me semi naked
cold wind blowing
for over an our
as externally I bear the indignity
trying to maintain nobility
as passerby's
look
gawk
but never stop
not even so called 'black' cop

At 4pm, I remain silent
and again that day
ask the Ancestors for guidance and protection
they lead me inside
and I retain my dignity
I don't want to hurt the other
I don't need to hurt the other

but the other wants to hurt me
the other feels it needs to hurt me
abuse me
incarcerate me
assassinate me
through me
and do crimes to me
until eventually I'll be free
eventually
eventually I leave force custody
home with family
sleep uncomfortably

and so I sit here this morning writing
wanting to cry
again
but the release wont flow
so I sit here writing
for a means to dispel the anger
but the spirit says no
and after libation
I suddenly know
I am not afraid
I am not afraid
I am ashamed
for they shame we

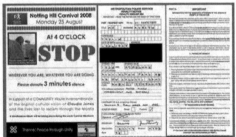

for until we no longer
pretend we are free
until we
when you see I
meaning we
meaning love
self above
me
liberation work
comes to an end
my so called friends, brothers, others..
you see
nothing hurts like betrayal
for betrayal is like no other hurt.

officer 491

'give it' shouts
officer 491
armed with his gun
scared at what I have done
capturing Truth
revealing what
he..
no what they..
have become
police officer – 4-9-1
danger
yet I do not run
dare not run
cannot run

illegal toll booth
taking from the road
gang of thieves
and no - not working alone

it's like being trapped inside a prison
only this time without that – ism
ethnicity, so called race, playing second place to crapitalism
in a space breathing so much beauty
yet my brothers still ignoring their duty
and in that tussle and bustle
as naija hussles
we seem to lose sight
of our spiritual muscle.

one won

We won he said
knowing one won
and the truth was
there was no we

too harsh to bear
he wanted to share
and so he did
ignoring the fact..

that the twos and threes hid
as he did their bidding
whilst the four and fives closed eyes
as they lied through their lives living?

as the six and the sevens
closed hands and prayed
for someone to save them
not him one
but that one
the one who enslaved and betrayed them

but the eight and nines tried
and that gave him the strength
to endure all the struggles
for the final length

and although the ten and eleven
took a long time coming
they were part of the one
an extension
a feeling of at last belonging

the one felt at ease
as twelve and thirteen arrived
for his new found family
had enabled him to survive

we won he said
and they all agreed
and as he passed on he knew
their legacy would survive he.

the cult
(seeking protection - from)

[Enter Shango. He rests having just returned from war. Suddenly he is confronted by Oya and Ògún. They attack...]

He called
she called
they called
softly softly then upon failure
ruthlessly, arrogantly devoid of harmony or grace,
violating his sanctuary, his space
spitting in his face
spiritual vitriol
from a pit of untruthal ritual

then suddenly like zombies they swarm
attacking first his then his families phone
he would not join their clan
holding hands
sharing plans
with naa poo
mama aboo
leader brother
sista vodun
queen mother [all hail she of the indigenous]
father elijah-khan [all hail he of the asiatic]
or any other
self defined
self imposed
charismatic leader
preacher
teacher

... "spiritual" ...

whilst simultaneously
violently unhumble
traditional healer
priest
imam
diviner
amengansie
babalowa

male
female
gatekeeper
whatever..

... praying
preying
all whilst ultimately demanding
... paying

for through ifayoma to the Ancestors we can see you...
all of you
"sincere" - yes
"honest" - no
they know
we know
he knows
she knows

"fear"

"egos"

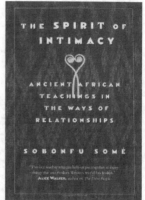

so in defeat
they returned
to that retreat
that "amazing" retreat
where the spirit of ababio
masquerades
as damfo
whilst dreaming it is densu
renewing
refocusing
its recruiting
where
the spirit of infantile jealousy
leads to their violation of intimacy
manipulative behaviour through unnecessary fear of rivalry
leading to their betrayal of Truth though the ash circle of intimacy

[Aunt Elegua screams, Oya screams]

they ignore his dreams where he guided by spirit screams;

"please just leave me alone"

leave me alone [Shango inside crying]
leave me
alone [Shango outside dying]

for at last
i am almost home [Shango spiritually smiling]
without
you.

[Shango curls his fingers around Oya's ear and Caresses. Exit Shango.]

the end (seeking closure - to)

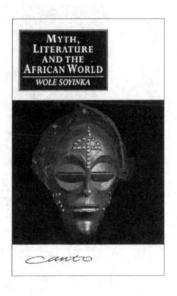

gone

And the resistance claims yet another ally
leaving me once again alone to face the struggle
raising questions of why I continue
as I continue
to lose all those around me who won't understand
nor take a stand
yet seeking my light
basking in my right
against those left
who benefit from my daily journey into the dark
who unforgivingly now feel to call me harsh
as i struggle maintaining a civil face
against an almost hopeless case
based solely on faith
to preserve our race
while I slowly lose sight
of my sanity?
well f u
and f
vanity.

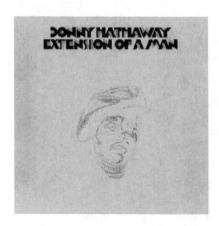

fatherly pain

I cried today,
it felt so strange,
i had to leave the room,
maintain my air of cool

it took me by surprise,
as hard as i denied,
i couldn't stop the flooding
from filling up my eyes

as i walked alone in pain
i thought about my son
my boy
my little baby
although if i call him that he won't agree

so what's the reason for me leaking?
the fears behind my tears?
i just received a phonecall
about a letter
at my home

she asked if she should read it
the legal stamp implied
a letter from the solicitor
yes "read me the reply"

she opened up the letter
each line was an event
i thought i must be dreaming
as i queried what it meant

with the subtlety of a hammer,
and the rodency of a rat,
the lies contained within the lies,
using our son as a bat.

clues

QUOTE
"And I saw a beast rise up out of the sea, having seven heads and ten horns, and upon his horns ten crowns, and upon his heads, the names of blasphemy. And they worshipped the dragon which gave power unto the beast: and they worshipped the beast, saying, "Who is like unto the beast? Who is able to make war with him?"

The Revelation of St. John the Divine, Chapter 13: Verses 1 & 4

The monster has spoken
and Johan lives
gaining strength
speech
preach
teach
leech
recruiting
training
desperately
preying on
vulnerable
naive
souls
leaking gold
manipulated
drugged by
tales of mystical odes
joining
blindly
till
slap
SNAP
wilfully
breaking families
killing souls
devouring
spirits
whole...
hole..
ho.

but, he also lives

phoenix like
rebirthed with life
a simple doctor, healer
teacher
seeking Truth
proof of
innocence
caught in a malicious act
devoid of facts
destiny
leading
no...
re-shaping his
path
towards
their main event
where war
awaits
and he
confronting
no..
releasing..
unleashing..
his inner self
protected as
evil tries
fights
but this time fate decides
ultimately dies
releasing souls as
sick weakened spirits
hide
cry
then fly
home
tragically
broken

at last..

Dr Kenzo Tenma has awoken.

tic toc

Tic toc, tic toc
im gonna explode in your face
if you do not stop
for too long have I marched for justice
whilst shouting loud about inequality
but do you even hear
what im saying
nah you just want me to keep praying
to you
and images of you
like an idol
an idle fool

tic toc, tic toc
im gonna explode in your face
if you do not stop
seems the only language you understand
is violence
not empty threats but real manifestations against oppression
see when i get aggressive without action
I sell myself and integrity short
with that fake reaction
and then comes the lies
when the truth is denied
yet some how you manage
to get us back on your side
where I walk on my knees
and begging you please
massa give free?

no... i refuse to be he, she, we

tic toc
tic toc
tic toc
boom.....

motherly love

An attack
like a knife in the back
but it came from the front
through my son
from his mom

feeling
paralysed
neutralised
perpetual
paternal
suicide

i dare not defend
for fear I strike
the innocent soul
my child
our child.

Ò) gún's crisis of identity

I feel shame
i knew me
but now the pain seeks to change and...
own me
and as my strength waynes
dark nights feel sane
evil is deforming
conforming
coming through me
seeking to maim
those outside the game
to end our reign
to increase our pain

so I bond with solace,
vulnerable from grief
and as I struggle from the casualty of normalcy
hope, now masked as fantasy
romance, an ancient intimacy
suppressing, violent emotion
repressing, eternal devotion
denying, the open wound
now an eternal tomb
driving my craft, my art
my bleeding heart...

i reflect

and see in you
an inhumane infidelity
damaging we
a collective body
torturing we
a soulless life
jealous of we
and in its misery,
severing links
providing we
safety, love and
family

and yet deep inside
through prides mask i hide
respected whilst dejected
achieving through leading
remaining
adama-nt,
a relentless, now defective detective
like Ògún, driven to battle
despite struggling to achieve
balance and
contentment

Healing

(afromantic dreams & relationships)

nwn

Peace, tranquillity
i sought, i found and now bound
within my spirit feels
a new energy, a new synergy
not only with physical self
but that wealth of health
that comes from rebirth
a grounded connection with the earth
as both sea and sun
recharge me
rejuvenate me
and brings purification of me
a chance once again to just be
the African child who sees beyond
the blue sky, sea,
red, gold and green
both tied yet freed with purpose
healed by elders
manifestation of Ancestors
empowered by ba,
moved with ib
invested with Ma'at
reconnected to the Creator,
Nwn.

the cliff

It was like falling
eyes shut
into a bottomless chasm
unpredictable
indescribable
free fall

time
rushing, pausing
and breathing
probing, exploring whilst
reaching, teasing

velocity, increasing,
resistance building,
compliance?
denial
fear even,
as i hit the floor
wanting
more....

the right story

Tell me about our Ancestors she said
not the pain, suffering, enslavement and degradation
but the work, triumphs,
and historical achievements
talk about the marvels of ancient civilisations
the bedrock of society
built from our foundations
share with me your thoughts on our deeds
not our needs
define us outside
that window of
violence,
victimhood
and slavery

and as she revealed the depths of her passion
as her eyes shone bright
my reaction
was not one of surprise
but delight
for I could see
her preparedness to fight
and I knew in that instant I was right
she was right
that flame in her eyes
couldn't deny
that beautiful soul
hidden inside
I smiled
and we paused for awhile...

both free for awhile
warmly exploring the other
spiritually journeying together
ignoring the
cold nights
wet and windy weather
for we were
two aries on opposite sides
two genders
two hearts

but of one mind
and as that brief moment of nakedness passed
the cool breeze
demanded a hug
we resisted
and continued to tease
but we knew
both knew
the other was free
for a situation that
mustn't be
so we laughed
and went into the night
feeling warm
feeling good
feeling right.

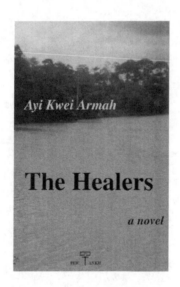

Ayi Kwei Armah

The Healers

a novel

PER TANKH

love we

I don't care if you're large, small
short or tall
for me to love you

"i must love me"

i don't care if your hairs short, braided
nappy or... hated
see, for me to love you

"i must love me"

i don't even care if you have a baby
as long as you carry yourself like a lady
cause for me to love you

"i must love me"

but i do care if you read
instead of living in front of that damn tv
and i do care that you dream
and believe one day we will be free
and i do care that you instinctively, unquestionably,
uncompromisingly, undeniably know...
a brothas arms is your home
yes i care,
and i fear,
to be alone....

so understand this...

i don't care if you're st lucian, nigerian, grenadian, ghanaian,
jamaican, zimbabwean because all are ONE with African
for me to love you

"i must love me"

i don't care what he said, what he did
he's in the past, history, now...
today you're with me
and for me to love you

"i must love me"

       for i don't care what they say
       as you are and always will be my... queen
       but....
       for me to love you...

"i MUST"
       please repeat....

"i MUST love me".

i remember...

Sweet
warm breath,
body
pressed close,
pulse
racing fast
heart
torn in half

eyes
wide shut
lips
stay untouched
words
thought un said
try
to pretend

what
cannot be
is
reality
last
eternity
pure
insanity

no.

friends remember
we remember,
I remember.

chat

What you doing?
she asked
i laughed
i was in bed
relaxed for once
and chilled
strangely feeling
fulfilled

and we talked
and it was good
as we broke boundaries,
tested realities,
challenged perceptions
whilst
debating deceptions
contradictions
making predictions.
with all but minor
interruptions.

what you doing?
i asked
she laughed
see she too was in bed,
guard lowered
truth flowered
as we
connected
thoughts,
fears, unprotected

as the minutes evolved
words became bold
stories told
secrets now known
trust was implied
as we delved deep inside
no reason, no motive,
it was just
a vibe.

talk

We need to talk I told him
but he pulled away as I tried to hold him
acting like my words were a weapon
my tears a lie
and my pain not real
but he did not want to talk,
he said
not now, but much later,
like there was an issue now more important
than this present,
than our future.

eating peanuts

As she looked back into him
she recognised
realised
he was
her one,
yes he was beautiful
but it was deeper
more romantic
their unquenchable addiction
had taught her
his sensuous touch
magnificent physique
could not compare
to his
incredible mind,
that vibe when they
spiritually
dined
entwined
united as one
almost indistinguishable as two

For she admired his soul,
his flow,
the way he
arrogantly always knows
her,
inside and out
upside and down
feeding her,
loving her,
and yet
she pondered
wondered
why
after three years
six months
fourteen days
and nine hours,
why
they
no longer woke,

nor spoke
together
forever
questioning
the cost of their
perfection
as he
left her
for the way she
nosily
ate
peanuts?

morning

We woke
and the dream was still real
it was you
in my arms as we talked
closed my eyes
seduced by a touch
joined your lips
unafraid to be home
passion spent
we smiled
sometimes cried
souls entwined
happy inside
as we dined
on a
promise of
lifetime
anew
morning darling
I love you.

the African Woman

I love her
the African woman
my physical reflection, my spiritual connection.
she who completes me
normalises and not exoticises me.
respects and not tolerates me,
challenges without embarrassing me,
educates without denigrating me,
loves me, and only me, for me being me.

please try to understand,
i am her man, not a money making fan.
please try to relate,
she is my woman, and not a feminine man.
i'm enslaved by devotion to emotions for her
i'm enraged by erosion of respect towards her
i'm engulfed by her aura of physical perfection
i'm enticed by her presence and her soul, intellect and...
i'm entwined in our struggle , which she recognises..
which she never denies is...
real

but we are Africans,
and we as Africans complement each other
choosing to
assimilate and integrate each other
unify and diversify each other
intensify and pacify each other
procreate and multiply as.... lovers
making perfect baby African others

we are...
jagged parts of the same whole
an African family
with high and lows
both equal and unequal
yet together as one
both weak and strong
and old with young

for if I am her sky
then she is my sun

and If I am her tree
then she is my roots
i smile for her
i cry for her
i live for her
and I'll die for her
for
unconditionally
i love her
the African Woman.

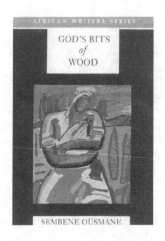

change (Pain)

I didn't change
but you did
it was hard to detect at first
little comments
suggestions, interventions
disagreement on previous grounds of unity
challenging spiritual and ideological directions
picking at my male inflections
painful yes
but still

i wouldn't change
not even when you took me for cleansing
i had faith and trusted you to protect me
till then you had never disrespected me
indicated sharing our intimacy
lied or deceived
or betrayed me
but still

i couldn't change
but we did,
less talk, more sex, more arguments,
less fun, more angst, more hurt
painful yes
but I held on
thinking we were strong
sensing i was wrong

i didn't change
but you did
and perhaps that was the problem
the more things stayed the same
the more you blamed
and desired
change.

inspire/desire

You inspired me to move, when my world collapsed
i couldn't breath, couldn't see, through the pain, tears and loss
you listened, without judgement, guided without taking sides
in fact it was the depth of your wisdom, that led me to notice your eyes

you see your outer beauty left me distracted,
and to my shame i even reacted
neglecting, my responsibility,
overjoyed by your assistance and kind hospitality
near abuse in any eventuality

i was blind, in my selfishness, i didn't first see you cry
but over time i came to realise, you too were hurting inside
in response i wanted to hold you, payback that which you gave to me
but i was so hungry, too needy, for your inner beauty - i became too
greedy

now the Ancestors have placed us away from each other,
discipline and spirit, not competing, but once again healing
and so we remain two friends facing crisis of vulnerability
it is time for reciprocity and that means spiritual generosity

so i'm torn trying to discover, how best to inspire
help you rebuild that world,
manifest your dreams as real
i want to be there as your friend
spiritual other, not physical lover
i want simply to inspire
irrespective of chemistry shouting - desire.

honey

Infuse with me
said peppermint
to sweet dripping honey
lips licking
contemplating (pleasuring)
warming
his tummy.

called

Why?
to say what?
did you need confirmation of that
victory?
yes its history,
I thank the Ancestors
for instilling pride in me
so I did not cry
then
as I died
and learn how to turn that corner
as I yearn for the pain to stop
the hurt to rot
and emotions fall back in order

did you call
cause you cared,
that you wanted me near
and couldn't bear
me bare
and feared
my tears?

or were you curious
part furious
spurned
and burned
in need to ensure
that the lesson was learned

I know you
knew you
cruel you
is not true you
so why did you call
to tell me you still love me
as you simultaneously
left me
alone
on the phone
broken
at home.

mind over fear

DISCIPLINE is everything.
see FREEDOM
contradicts
unrestricts
and enables us to share
a burden we would bear
mind over fear
should PASSION
bring us together
tearing
us
apart
into
restrictive
physical
yet sensuous
sexual CAPTIVITY

therefore
is being true
truly being
entwined in each other's mind
FLYING
curious
of what we'll find
ignoring the truth
that it is the SPIRIT that binds
the physical
and once BOUND
could break
if forced to unwind?

rewind?

NO.
honesty
integrity
shall have to GUIDE
for I cannot fear nor deny
that impulsive you
nor suppress
the reckless me

that I know
we know
and continue to CONTROL
as she-he innocently grows
from
natural curiosity
spiritual reciprocity
based on
TRUST in
you and
me.

departure

Sad he departs
still happy for he sees
her art
her naked
mischievous heart.
she glides,
quietly yet not hiding
moving... no... dancing
painting a picture
richer not just for her grace
but also her building sensual pace

her form empowered by rhythms
driven by spiritual visions
leaving sweat on a beautiful melanated canvas
forming drops of squarecircles
dripping emotions extending her loving
creative
rage

yet, her steps mask her pain
her our i we he me shame
for the collective voices have faded
memories idly invaded
liberatory passions
jaded by
distorted expressions of cold death
masqurading as warm breath

some do not see nor feel her
and in fear made greed seek to steal,
to supress...
her future,
her present,
her presence,
her devine
essence

but beyond words the music inspires
her dreaming remedies
forming freedoms partners'
new language of melody

'dance...'
'dance with.... '
'dance with me'

she inhales
here
now
aloud 'not allowed' they say
but their body muscles twitching betrays
so she smiles,
singing...
i'm alive
we're alive
don't - be - a - lie

be
alive
teasing
but never misleading
pleasing
without undignified pleading
romancing an earth experience
motivated by...
...spirit.

my sister

I tried to write a poem
about how much I love her so
but I just couldn't find the words,
verbs, nouns or sounds

you see this in-tonal language makes it hard
to express
the profound,
intense
joy of having her around
inside of my life
outside of my strife
and within
all that's right
in the circle of me

see she
grounds me
nurtures me
heals me and
simply loves me
all me
warts, faults,
and all,
even when I feel
I'm not deserving
of that love.

see she,
supports me,
teaches me,
laughs at me and with me
makes me feel I'm naughty
but never faulty
on those occasions I
stray from that path
every once in awhile
and when awhile's all at once
and im alone
from decisions
and isolating missions

that require
strong positions...

she's there
all there
always near
despite her fears.

and so I think about her smile,
her quick wit,
suppressed fits
as she hides
all inside
when she's playing
to catch those who
underestimate
and therefore
make the bad mistake
of trying to abuse
her kindness
with bad mindness...
I get sad,
then mad,
the only way to calm myself is to
think about her warm embrace
her beautiful face
which gives me faith
and guides me back
when I cry
or die inside
lost in a
world
so hostile
it makes me want to
curl into a ball
weep and then
sleep
deep

and so as I try and write a poem
about my sister
I think about my mother,
sister
and all those others
who have missed her

for in our parents gift to we
in creating she
the only word
I think that can
express what I mean is
ife.
I love her,
my sister.

n'factor

What is it?

why do only few of us have that ability to listen
then talk and walk that talk at the same time,
make you belly laugh with truth humour
when you just want to curl up inside and cry

innocently, tease and pleasing our spirit
technically, expertly massaging our wounds,
willingly, extending warmth and compassion
when it's in fashion to only care for the I

it's a naturally, nurturing relationship,
with an organically natural shy high,
what is it that drives the n'factor
where the rest of us would not even try.

she saved me

When i was in pain
thought i'd never love again
she - held - me
she told me
if i was insane
then she would remain
chained to me
dedicate her life with..
but not to me
recognise our needs
and grow to subsume me

I needed that
for i'd lost my ability
to see beyond
what others saw in me
became enslaved to my heart
unshackled
and in return
allowed others to abuse me
but she soothed me

Me

I speak much of me
and little of we
how together we
share a space others want
although they can't relate
why imprisoned here
i willingly accept this fate
for in return
I try not to deny
the normality
masquerading as our spiritual high
to realise i am able to fly
because although i may guide
she has painstakingly prepared the physical ride
she saved me
setting we
free.

lil'mzstuch

Her
cool,
hot fire
burning without heat
passion
masking thoughts
as she smiles
disarming
charming..

..him
the forceful hurricane
pulled by her teasing
gently easing
with deliberate ignorance
a thunderous confidence
leaving him
willingly
helpless
intoxicated by
her smoke and flames
his fire and rain
and yet after both taste
that delicious pain
where danger often feeds
personal gain
she starts
dreaming of her next reign
of coolly burning hot
once again.

my man

My man loves me for me,
and tells me so
shows me so
wants me so

yes I may cook and clean for him
but he's willing to learn
yes, the food he cooks is occasionally burned.
but my gratitude is earned

my man loves me for me
and tells me so
shows me so
wants me so

he calls my name whilst I watch him sleep
pulls me close when he sees me weep
yes I love my man more than life.
wish his father would just call tonight.

embrace

With the gentleness of a spiders web
he silently felt her..
warm, sincere
far and yet
so near
without prompt
nor ceremonial pomp
a dream?
no its real,
and for that brief moment...
with that..
oh so tender...
movement
they were both free
sharing skin
touching thoughts
through
innocent
means.

froze

He froze
scared to respond
his body closed
for she could not know
what he did..
that his attraction to her
was too big..
and so he hid
whilst savouring the caress of
her touch
desperate to reciprocate
but maintaining discipline whilst yearning
her touch
his spirit poised to dominate
and consume because of
that touch
so he froze
and with that pause
she turned from
nice
to
ice.

light

Quietly she observers
questioning only if
she does not disturb
learning through
listening to words
that turn
her minds
focus onto
thoughts unheard

silently
she involves herself
through actions
she evolves their-selves
'crastination turns to action
eventually casting light
where once was darkness
now a path
towards
obtaining
quality of
life.

'fro

At last she revealed herself
soul at ease
hair unleashed
holding breath
taking risks
trusting him
as they fell
without sound
eventually touching ground

and in return
she opened
passion unrestrained
sharing lessons learned
and in so doing
transforming views
creating new
a richer picture
of a young and
deeper
sista.

purple

Is beauty a puzzle our mind creates
an answer that helps us find that space
where our dreams are made real
manifested as infantile matter
emotional energy
raw spirits together

is beauty that desire to kiss your lips
or the detour from breathing
as a heartbeat skips
where quiet words unsaid
become deafening loud
and attraction is oblivious of any crowd

is beauty us talking with eyes so wise
or sensuously sharing the air
inhaling Truths inside
accepting and respecting
being free to just be
and in that synchronised moment
uniting as,
we

is beauty embracing you're unique like no other
or wanting and loving you
each meeting anew
penetrating the facade
of hard shell like defences
surrendering to a purple heart
devoid of pretences.

you

Who were you that came into my life
from my life
who were you that gave me life
through your life
who were you that life denied
a longer time
in this our life
i cried
for
we
are
you.

nursery – I

What's her name?
said the cute little boy
as he offered her a toy
eyes full of joy
but my daughter was shy
and ignored his advance
yet as she clung to my side
there were signs...
...of a smile.

nursery – II

As we said bye
she cried
blocking the door
as tears hit the floor
she looked round for her coat
but like a true sentry
she blocked entry
to the exit
and as she stood there she gazed
searching mums eyes, then i's eyes
for the glimmer of a sign

the sign WE would go
but with her in tow
but i had to say no
so she cried
she cried
mum picked her up
she was soothed by her touch
but as she went down
feet touching the ground
she knew...

yes, she knew
it was time for us to go
she ran to my arms
so i asked for a kiss
then a hug
she complied, briefly smiled, and then.....
gave up
as i put her down gently
she cried again
this time walking away with her new playmate
as she resigned
with signs...
...of a smile.

Random

(3, 2, imagine)

information

What if ..
all energy is kinetic information
and we all only exist to process that information
and those who live do so by transforming that information

what if..
every action can be expressed as a transmission of information
every dream and desire a manipulation of that information
every truth or lie based on interpretations of that information

what if..
we've valued ourselves by the quantity of that information
instead of valuing ourselves on the quality of that information
instead of liberating ourselves by sharing and spreading, raw
information

what if
an artist is a person who manipulates old information
a consumer a person who assimilates new information
and commerce the means to dilute and pollute... all information

what if..
our future is the persistence of true historical information
our children are simply the transformation of genetic information
whether we live or die is based on free movement of that information

information is power?

or is power.... information?

free poetry

"free poetry" shouted the poet,
the people were confused,
for the poet had no samples,
no leaflets, no products for them to consume

"free poetry" said the poet,
"where's the book?" the people ask,
"where's the CD?... where's the website?"
"where's the literature for me to view?"

"free poetry" whispered the poet,
words reflecting heart and soul,
commercial prostitution?
a divorced parent from its birth

"free poetry" cried the poet,
"a dream, I don't believe"
the poet cried till a lone voice said,
"that's why we don't succeed"

"free poetry" sang the poet,
released from all its chains,
conceived from spiritual motives,
is true, is pure is freed...

©the world

maths

I used to think it a universal language
or so they taught me
a collection of digits based on
existence and
non existence
persistence of patterns
forming clusters,
defining formulas
derived from equations

no half truths, lies or anomalies
just truths
but one is not always = to 1
apparently some ones are > others.

free thought

Free thought
I think
without a price
as I entice them to escape
whilst
dreaming dreams
as I'm awake
of themes I try
to leave to fate

free thought
a skill that
can't be taught
a mind that
can't be bought
an opinion that is
always sought
by
enclosed minds.

nice poem

If you want to take a dagger and stab it in my heart
then tell me that my poetry is nice
you see that pat on the back
is a virtual slap
so let me start again
and this time...
listen close
my passive activist friend.
if my poetry is 'nice',
then I have failed in my mission
i seek justice not contrition,
i promote revolution
not absolution.

my words are meant to change the way you think,
to challenge your perception,
tear down political, cultural and media deceptions.
when Chinua cried out 'Beware Soul Brother',
his rhythm created a venue for future dancers,
future others, dreamers and lovers
and when Ken Saro-Wira left us after shaping the melody
the oppressive mantra 'nice poem' was convicted.

a 'nice poem' of...
no fixed ideological abode,
was,
found guilty,
of demeaning,
persistent expressions of poetical resistance,
in an all African court,
deliberated by a jury devoid of prejudicial
venal
artistic
bias.

this is NOT a 'nice poem'.

silence

I raped her
then nothing happened
there was this...

...silence

who am i
what am I that I would defile
she of those who gave birth
to me
and we
was it a moment of lunacy
or a part of my destiny
can I excuse
that I took away her right to choose
that I forced her to accept my abuse
in response for rejecting my love noose

she now looks at me with a hatred
I have never seen before
a ferocity I have never felt before
yet she felt my power
I say it is our love I want to recover
but now she only want to shower
she cries for hours

he raped me
then nothing happened..
silence...

how could it be
this violent
spiritual monstrosity
borne
from death of reciprocity
can exist in a world
where
preachers claiming healer status
kneeling
praying
then ultimately preying
on mother, sister

and even baby
daughter
lead then leave their women to the slaughter

father confess your sins
my brother confess your sins
but no
before only god you say
denying that you have lost your way
our way
the way
as you betray all that you say
we are

CONFESS

but there is only...
... silence

yet, you were not silent
when driven by flesh
ego manifest
you violated my sacred womb
desecrated my spiritual place
where once was love
is now hate
so brother sister
can no longer relate
as I try to overstand the reason
why I feel disgraced
and socially find
my compassion is now misplaced
true love is hard to face
i fear betrayal in its place

.. SILENCE...

i raped her
maybe what I did wasn't so wrong
the silence says its privilege of the strong
yet why do I wake at night seeing her in my dreams
with daytime echoes of her screams
no meaning yes
in that beautiful dress
perhaps there's nothing for me to confess

he raped her
then there was..
..silence

....and as a woman cried, the community died.

priceless

The best things in life are free
unless you try to turn them
into a commodity
then for a fee
we can make believe
a purchase is the act
of owning freedom legally.

rain

Rain reigns
when it pours around me
through me
into me
when its purr
invades me
drowns me
consumes me

rain reigns
when our lips kiss
skin pressed together
teasing
needing
feeding
a magical moment forever
cosmologically
reflecting
connecting us
together

when i look up
and view light refracted
through our skylight
making love
romancing the earth
meditatating
invoking a spiritual rebirth
lifes bittersweet pain
is for a moment
all washed away
as rain
reigns

Urbanodity

(the early years)

bLACK anthem

urban education

Massa say work hard and i be free
and i believe dem and dey democracy
for he and she are kind 2 we
make sure we eat and they no more beat

massa say i learn i earn
if i be good i move out of hood
he no teech me how 2 reed and rite
i dance and sing and he say i bright

massa say Africa iz bad
backwoods culture, language dere
he teach me inglish not mumbo sounds
dis way I can stand up pwoud and bow

massa say I came from land
where dirty, poor means aids and wars,
dey have no food or money dere
dat's why African want 2 come here

massa give me nice new name
his Ancestor history from whence it came
so i no more African see i is bLACK
and i thank my lord massa's god for dat

politics of hair

urban image

Now when a sista grows her hair out,
there's this expectation for her to shout
for many she embodies the stereotype of the radical
who stands up proud and loud for her family
her community
our
queen

but if that same sista cuts her hair short,
some assume feminist
or lesbian thoughts
others think African through a monolithic veil
where shes a savage, untamed,
purely sexual game.

when she grows her hair natural
some call her and says its nappy,
they claim that she can't be happy
they can't understand that she's in complete
and total love with her African self

it's like when a brotha walks around wearing an afro
all of a sudden there's places he cant go
all because he said no
when they tried to cut down and trim his African halo

but when a sista attacks her head with chemicals
attacking her roots,
while undoing those curls
removing character in place of bland uniformity
wearing it long and straight in an act of soulless conformity
they claim that now she's beautiful
She's no longer ugly
no longer typical
cause her hair and thoughts are relaxed
mind and body receptive
to a cultural invasion that they know will ultimately makes her
defective

a strong blond tint

unnatural and shouting
brotha I'm still mad atcha
what could it mean?
this urban dream
where brothas dye their mane blond,
celebrated as new queens
as they parade in their political,
asymmetrical folical based thongs
doing wrong,
real wrong.

home
urban myths

Trouble, they claim
as they
misbehave
and
play away
and
find excuses
for reasons why they don't want to go...

attitude, they bray
as they
fail to meet those
simple feats of
standing tall, understanding all
of the
mirrored issues
that reflect their
dreams
and
subsequent realities
their
entwined
totally related destiny

love, they sing
as they
squirm and hide
with that
unconscious pride
and deny all the facts
of their consistent acts
when we know
that they've simply
lost their way
home

123

urban unity

I talk of i
how i
think and
i want and
i need
i cry

i sigh
i hope you buy
what i
did as i
feel i
love i

whilst "they"
talk of we
no sign of... me
pure
he and
she
in unity

they celebrate
and originate
thoughts
that
breed
freedom and
liberation
salvation
and
self determination

i..
me..
we..
free.

broken word
urban theft

And so it begins
that creative sin
of mimicking our African american cousins
as poets mimic inflections
choosing new yorkian intonations
over home grown, cultural innovation
under estimating their worth
their unique identity cultivated from birth
thoughts delivered, spoken as
rhythmically, dancing words.

that song
urban entertainment

Do you love me? she whispered
as he sat there listening to that song,
whilst the women in the video paraded their thongs,
collectively all doing her sistren wrong.

fckd
urban relationships

He fucked me then left me
alone in MY home
when asked when id see him said
"wait by the phone".

footballer

urban icons

The man said i was too sensitive
so i punched him in his face
something about me having no integrity
for always dating outside my race
im english, black and proud
hey you? why you laughing out loud?
you're just jealous of my fame
what you mean aint I ashamed?

behind

urban fantasy

Hmm i wouldn't kick him out of bed she mumbled
as she spied on his naked behind
she glanced up and down his torso
oh yeah she said "he, is so fine"

i wonder if rumours are true,
she thought, as she dreamed of her fantasy ride
he moaned and groaned from feeling passion
as her hand slipped, exploring inside

as he saw the green light meaning action
ken told her "hold on...let me drive"
and as the poster shrunk into the distance
barby sighed "what a cute.. brown... behind"

stext

neo-urban philosophy

Da best aurl sx isnt a mouth gvng hd ona bed, but instd being fed, wid deep lyrcs, wrds said. buck u on fbk. peace.

consumarality

urban sales

Buy me, consume me,
exhume me then
re-
digest

target me, categorise me,
thereby qualifying me,
for a
funding-
stream

assimilate me, then sanitise me,
process my core essence make a
for-
tune

debase me, evaluate me, enslave me
thereby making
your
moral
tomb

bLACK and urban
urban and bLACK

Back in the day

black...
was cool,
was dark,
was true,
was real,
but now, now they say he's.... urban

a feud,
a duel,
of multi hues,
black lost,
and now they say she's.... urban

blond hair,
under turban,
blue eyes with
brown skin,
is now what it means to be.... urban

but what of poor black?

who was cool,
dark and true,
yeah fe real,
obsolete, like a negro, is sub... urban.

right on white

urban support

Right on white told us
he was in our liberation struggle
bemused
we listened
not wanting to burst his bubble

you see,
right on white claimed
our leaders as part of his struggle,
sharing his plight
uniting our fight
confusing
his invisible ism's
with our
unequivocal
social and
economic
prisons

right on white
heart in right place.
problem is
racial discrimination is not a concept
to which he could
nor should,
ever equate

yes,
right on white
needs to support our struggle,
but without need to claim,
name,
nor historically maim,
in need of fame

right on white
back off 'black'
yes,
forever sympathise,
but understand,

you can never
ever,
truly
empathise
with African.

backing black

urban politics

They say they back me cause i'm 'black',
thinking a change of shade
equals a change of game
but if the playas the same
if the rules aint changed
if the only colours
are black and white
options state - unite or fight

but not as an African
with a freedom agenda
and a spiritual centre
rising above
the role of dissenter
loyal to the people,
the Ancestors,
lover of papa
mama
Africa
home

but instead as a well suited image
of zombie like status
an exotic erotic
intellectual romantic
a potent distraction
a violent refraction
of truth
willingly
parroting
patriotic
rhetoric
of hope
like a pope
reinforcing fake religions
like a pimp
prostituting female divinity
in the name of debauch capitalist civility
in truth
an agent of deferred pornographic liberal inhumanity

not even standing as an African
not as we
not even for we
but as a 'coloured'-in-version
of what they aspire we to be
same politics
same vision
same demons
new revisions

if we still cannot see
beyond that trickery
overstanding our history
of neo colonial puppetry
then sure you back me because i am so called 'black'
but when you wake up
you'll still be under attack

Awakening

(politrix and injustice)

if

What if this life I'm living is a lie
a mask of normalcy
perpetrating a veil of pseudo reality
and what if my happiness is faked...
a refracted projection of my real world.
but all the while
my dreams of freedom
remain hidden
behind the illusion
confused by the truth
at ease with denial
eternally disturbed
as my conscious forever questions my fate
will I live?
forever dying?
this lie long life?

the day the lie died

I used to believe in democracy
Ignoring all its hypocrisy
until one day I woke
and realised it was a mockery
this state run 'peoples' democracy.
see in this democracy mob rules
there's no truth and justice for all
majority votes suppress the rest
while minority voices shout and are systematically oppressed.
corporate media informs the agenda
ignoring the fact that it's the worst offender
politicians lie and people die,
people die and yet the majority never really question why

why?

why in a system representing the people
is there no party that truly represents or protects all of the people?
why in a land of free speech and topical debate
is the most vote winning strategy to use racial hate?

how?

how in the worlds largest western democracy,
did a tyrannical dynasty legally manage to get re-selected, re-elected,
resist, persist and despite global condemnation
and a majority world rejection
continue by installing insecure satellites of its corrupting self?

meanwhile...

espousing propaganda of its social and moral health,
by abusing its fraudulently gained African sourced economic wealth.

who shall speak of the overt resource hungry imperialistic ambitions,
the unaccountability, lack of transparency,
the immoral elected politicians bereft of all responsibility
whilst the new world order baits nothing but fear,
loathing and hate,
as we wait for the emperor to decree its time
for an 'open and honest' debate

how? why?

because when true democracy died,
no-one cried
no, no actually that's not true
the minority cried...
and majority sighed,
then replied...
'its time to move on'
and truth and justice
were left outside.

now go hide.

an uncivil war

She, he or in most case me
can't you see
the truth is WE
both not free
together they're oppressed as one
divided by lies
designed to
keep them
from
the others side

when instead
united they must fight
not he plus one
nor she minus he
for his freedom is
their liberation
and her interdependence
is their salvation
not damnation
nor cause for
condemnation
and gender
relegation
separation

SEPERATION

this war
this.. uncivil war
that threatens to stop
nation building
and preaches us hate for
Africa's children
must STOP

STOP

a truce be drawn
relationships formed
new soldiers spawned
and a army borne

that fights for OUR rights
for justice
and then a world where
all Africans are treated
equal amongst themselves
for it is then
and only then
when we measure ourselves
against our greats of before
and make changes
challenging our own flaws
it is then
will we find
peace and justice
PEACE and JUSTICE
borne from our
unity
and self determined duty
to bring about the worlds
first and only
civil
evolution...

and gender
REVOLUTION.

civilised, developed, and democratic

It was the 'civilised' world that en-slaved us,
raped, and continues to restrain us
kings labelled bucks,
as our queens gave birth to new europe,
families sold as negro product ranges,
whilst communities were swapped for tobacco and labelled...
...stock

it is the 'developed' nations that de-trade us,
whilst continuing to economically short change us
diamonds sold
crude oil exported
resources stolen
till food stocks are now...
... barren

it was 'first' world people who de-faithed us,
using deities to justify degrading us,
our customs of old,
barbaric we're told
teaching, preaching, enforcing christianity
with the magic of science..
..and gunpowder

but it was *their* democracy that finally betrayed us,
funding regimes, polluting our dreams,
sending us aid, blocking our trade,
exporting our goods, importing their junk,
exotic guilt free vacations, as long as you please keep us locals at bay,
asylum, immigration, What problems?
begat annoyance, and now breeds severe....
......irritation.

richer minority, poorer majority

Why is research into helping the majority ills,
reduced coz the patients wont be ringing cash tills,
why the need for viagra,
over aids and tb,
profit driven neglect,
western greed before need?

25 in 24

25 million in 24
in 48 it was 50 tall
as cries of make poverty history
was sang mantra like by all
feed the world they played
its xmas time they brayed
give generous, its human
as 3 mill was barely gained.

aid

Humanitarian aid
international paid
democratic aid
military paid
financial aid
capitalism paid.
cure or virus
saved or paid
aid or aids?

state revenge

Hit us
and we'll, hit you back
scare us
and we'll, launch attacks
passing laws
revealing flaws
as we
march to war.

jobseeking

A system designed to intimidate,
infuriate,
humiliate
as I queue for my third appointment,
exam paper in hand,
reducing me as a man.
to fifty four pounds a week
as long as I seek
i weep
whilst creeping out the back door
hand outstretched forced
to beg once more.

democrazy falls

Only a fool believes in democracy
and the hypocrisy of aristocracy
where only the few can afford 'equality'
as they peddle the 'dream' of meritocracy

only a fool believes an election
is determined by the electorate
whilst the true campaign money of corporates
eclipses gdp's of the global unfortunate

only but,
fools believes that its the tool that deceives..
that in a world of political science,
with characters borne from media giants
that it's, legitimate for a nation of millions
to be represented by only three candidates
so who is the tool...
when...dem all crazy fools?

paedo files?

They knew,
they
all knew
but decided to suppress
in hope he confessed
to his
sins of all sins
his history, his destiny?

they knew,
they
all knew
that he abused
just for fun
but instead of persistence
for criminal conviction,
they weeded his files,
so in schools he could... smile?

they knew
they
all knew
yet their actions protect
instead of suspect
as these bureaucrats talk
and inquiries launched
and old records are torched
whilst justice is bought?

they knew
they
all knew
that these paedo files show
what it is we all know
that the rich and the famous
who say please do not blame us
for their sexual perversions
and moral diversions
whilst politicians betray us
as the media says "tell us"
whilst our children say "help us"
as the adults say "love us"

as the churches say nothing
while their agents are preaching
role model misuse,
through physical abuse,
as the schools now have laws
teaching cross gender 'contact'
and these 'civilised' stores
sell panties and bras
for children of six,
nah, they don't miss a trick,
this must be a fix,
hiding those who have power
whilst our young watch and cower
as the public consumes
whilst the truth is exhumed
in the grand court of flaw?

guilty?

inquiry?

in them we should trust?

....and then we all cry
let out a big sigh,
whilst another child dies
victim of a
dormant
paedo file?

the racists are gone

The racists are gone yet still i'm not free
what does this mean?
what else could it be?
why is it i....
still cannot see,
my... opportunities,
my... ambitions and dreams
in this reality.

the racists are gone and yet still i'm not free
to simply just be
and reach what i see
to share life with we
while we love who is me
still
injustice and pain
remain like a stain?

the racist are gone yet damn i'm not free
they said this was good
as they unmasked the hoods
like I knew that they would
when we showed that they could
and not because that they should.

and yet...

the balance of power
remains like a tower
of money and greed
deciding by creed
rejecting our needs
maintaining the seed
of the system devised
to deny and divide
based on race?

inequality rules in its place?

the racists are gone and still im not free,
for nothing is free in this
democracy.

truth holes

They court him
then caught him
now a
withered husk
broken
with no fuss
surrendering his infamy
as gloves
surgically dissect
and
inspect him
for mass
media consumption

His open mouth
shouts
indignity
whilst his
unkempt hair
beard now mane
screams
pity me

His power now
all gone
for
so long
done wrong
his evil omnipotence
revered
then reversed
now rehearsed
by the mockery
of democracy
of the peoples new
liberators
celebrators
his former
decorators

supporters,
installers of

regimes of haters and
dictators
for
unethical political favours
and yet...

his previous
friends and allies
now his
foes
with tales of
woes
who although have switched sides
deny all claims
that they
lied

they lied.

whole truths they cry
whilst like
during his reign
of terror and brutality
throughout their campaign
of shock and awe totality
remain guilty
of reporting
distorting
the human loss
in terms of regime costs

as...
uncounted innocents die
whilst few observe as
families cry
until
with a yawn
at red dawn
woken at their insistence
from a dream fight
with "no resistance"
nor pictures
of capture
in a war
of technological

psychological
propaganda
like the fairytale
saving lynch....
"we got him..."
trapped in a hole,
led by a mole
and truth holes.

road to segregation

You know those
status symbols
you parade in front of us
taunting us
reminding us
that you're elite

those mechanised wheels
enclosures of steel
with abs
gps

well hell we know where you are
there's no satellite required
the message is clear
you're the star
not the car

and we the observers
on buses and trains
on foot in the rain
are fooder to blame
when we scratch
dent your fame
maim your claim
to that road
of segregation.

hate crimes more likely

It's cold,
i think i'm going to have to wear a hat
and then i pause
as i considered
the possible consequences
of
this
act.

my belly rumbles,
i cant step out..
not without
a
little
bite,
i stop,
i yam,
damn,
now i'm late

my spar calls, where are you?
i'm at the station,
huh.. i lied..
the trains
delayed?
i'm on my way,
have patience
i soon come

another rumble, a real big rumble,
the train its almost here,
"gotta go"
blabs the phone, i run,
i run,
i run
i run

stop!

stop he said.
now i'm really looking vexed,
i'm breathing hard,

looking mad,
as my train now pulls
away.

what's the hurry, where's the fire?
he asks, in a sarcy tone
but as I start to explain,
i see her,
a woman crying.
and she's pointing
yes
i'm to blame

he was 'black',
with a hat,
yes
one that looked
just
like
that

my eyes open up with surprise
another car
stops,
another bro
pops

and i'm taken away
... in chains.

Notes

MAAFA

hope
Dedicated to the memory of Tajudeen Abdul-Rahim who said; "There is always something to be done. It can be changed. No matter how bad the situation is, it can be made better."

Written and inspired following a conversation with a friend discussing the perceived hopelessness of achieving African Liberation in our lifetime. At the time parliamentary corruption in the UK was at a all time high with politicians exposed as claiming extraneous expenses at the public expense and yet all of them escaping justice in contempt of the electorate. Meanwhile the attack on African people residing and arriving to the UK continued with the introduction of racist policies designed to block 'non EU' migrants from entering the UK.
9 June 2009.

insane
Written on the morning of my trial where I was prosecuted by the British state for obstructing their police force in the execution of their duty for actions which possibly saved the life of a young African in their custody. I now face the prospect of being criminalised by the state and facing three months in prison.
11 August 2008

i was abducted by aliens
A tribute to the literary genius Octavia Butler, who placed the idea in my mind of Maafa being so incredible to believe as reality, it could successfully be written as science fiction. She joined the Ancestors on 24 February 1996, an extremely talented and humble woman who despite the opportunity to flaunt or be motivated by wealth, devoted her life to both her family and work and in so doing became a role model for me.

plantation
In September 2003 I resigned from a well paying job in IT to work full time for the Pan African community, by establishing and building the Ligali organisation. Many African people continue to keep the history of Maafa alive by incorporating it in their daily language. Modern day use of the word plantation also refers to the economic enslavement system known as wage slavery or a job with absolutely no prospect of facilitating social mobility.

4
B4 our contact with europe we were Africans. But over 400 years of deliberate cultural disinheritance where we have been stripped of language, culture, religion and identity has convinced generations of African people in the Diaspora that they are 'black' and that Africans on the continent are 'black' Africans. The myth continues.

made in Africa
Inspired by the article *Another World is Possible for Africa* written by Pan Africanist scholar-activist Ama Biney on our collective responsibility to realise a progressive vision of leadership for Africa and her children wherever we are.
7 August 2009

slave name
In the Observer newspaper, 23 November 2003, the noted playwright Kwame Kwei-Armah wrote about how by the age of 12, he was sufficiently culturally politicised to start talking about discarding his 'slave name', which eventually he did, inspired by Alex Haley's *Roots* and the works of Malcolm X (El-Hajj Malik el-Shabazz).

From rejecting the label 'black' and using the word African to reclaiming a traditional African name by severing and burying family labels maintaining the odious legacy of the enslavers of our Ancestors, these remain some of the ways we continue to do justice to the memory of those who came before us.
23 November 2003

rant
We are constantly labelled by apathetic people comfortable with accepting their position in an inequitable society as complainers instead of campaigners simply seeking freedom. The sheeple argue that working to transform a system of oppression is futile so why don't we focus on much more important stuff instead, this ranges from why don't we keep our oppressors happy to lets secure a better position in the

system that deliberately denies freedom and dignity to others. Their belief is that raising awareness of injustice through protest achieves nothing whilst they themselves advocate nothing except - rants.
19 November 2004

march
As we attended the annual *united family and friends campaign* march, we were saddened by the lack of urgency, lack of priority given to the issues. The march ended up being an exercise in civil obedience when perhaps more would have been achieved if the several hundred people who attended said enough was enough and hinted that political inaction could lead to civil unrest.
Saturday 25th October 2003

dreaming revolution
Revolution is a word that means making change, to imagine that a racist will change without being forced to is to be dreaming, to engage in impotent debates about the classism and socio-economic inequality that has existed for hundreds of years is to maintain the myth. To achieve real revolution requires action not more talk, everything else merely obstructs its path.

struggle
Survival fatigue is a term I use to define the reality of our struggle to exist while draining us of the energy to invoke revolution.
1 January 2004

words hurt
I was lied to as a child. Words do hurt. Fortunately they can also be used to educate, to motivate, to liberate.

shut the back up
Inspired by my return visit to online African British forums and witnessing an epidemic of what can only be described as irrelevant apathetic cyclic debate criticising without offering solutions the very people raising awareness of injustice. It made me realise that if our Ancestors like Harriet Tubman, Kwame Nkrumah, Malcolm X or Marcus Garvey were with us today, many of us would fail to support their revolutionary work.
12 December 2003

WOUNDED

betrayal
Written following my arrest and imprisonment at Notting Hill Carnival on Bank Holiday Monday where I was injured in an unprovoked attack by several Notting Hill Carnival security staff after giving a BBC 1xtra DJ a flyer asking for him to support a united call for three minutes silence in remembrance of our Ancestors. I sustained bruising to my head where I was repeatedly punched. None of the assailants were arrested. They were all African.
26 August 2008

officer 491
After observing officers from the Nigerian police force stopping motorists and taking cash from them I am assaulted and subject to an attempted kidnap at gunpoint. I was saved after my friend Yomi Oloko (head of DIFN) caught up with the officers after chasing them down the road in car and on foot and directly challenged the legality of the operation taking place.
22 January 2010

one won / gone / tic toc
*Why the f*** do I bother collection*
The pressure of liberation work is often very intense, the threats on life very real, intimidating and scaring all around and despite mass public support often leaving those in leadership naked, vulnerable and feeling very lonely. Sometimes, during moments of reflection the decision to give public credit to others for victories achieved at great risk and sacrifice to self very difficult but it's for the greater good. I give thanks to Emma Pierre-Joseph & Shaka Marday who at the time of my despair unexpectedly gave me hope.
12 August 2005

the cult
Inspired by Tarell Alvin McCraney Yoruba infused play "In the Red and Brown Water", after the successful first ever broadcast of Nyansapo - The Pan African Drum. On the eve of broadcast the warnings I received against launching the station escalated as the instigators revealed their true identity to me. The launch show was a tribute to the late Miriam Makeba

who crossed over to the Ancestors on 10th November 2008, the discussion topic was "Is it wrong to mix art and politics?"
19 November 2008

clues

After I experienced a barrage of personally crippling physical and spiritual attacks from unexpected quarters, the healing teacher element of my spirit was forced to awake to temper an Ògún response. Inspired by sinister real life events and the powerful anime series based on Naoki Urasawa's "Monster".

Ògún's crisis of identity

This was written the following morning after re-watching the Casino Royale (2006) film. My deepest fears stem not from attacks upon myself but from the risk posed to my family and friends by enemies targeting them because that are unable to break my spirit. The story of Ògún, the African Orisha with whom I am most connected to and the DC graphic novel on this theme *Identity Crisis* reflects this, hence the title.

Raised in the UK I originally grew up admiring the strength of character in fictional heroes like Captain Kirk, James Bond, William Adama (BSG 2004), Wolverine, Peter Parker, Hal Jordan, Clark Kent, the Black Panther and my favourite comic book hero – Bruce Wayne. Although as an adult I have now adopted real life African role models both female and male, today, many of these fictional personalities have left a permanent scar within my psyche. Yet whilst many have sought to bestow the title of leader upon me, like Ògún, I have always rejected the notion preferring to be recognised an African providing leadership in the field I work.

But now as I look at myself, I can see the price of my commitment to liberation work has been high. Throughout 2010, for the first time in my adult life I lost focus, I stopped training (Africentred martial arts - *Maashufa*), cycling and swimming. These are all the essential activities that kept my body in tune with my spirit. As a result I put on physical weight, consumed foods that contained unhealthy additives and most days awoke feeling slower, weaker, emotionally and physically exhausted.

Don't get me wrong, I was still working, indeed my mind was fully engaged at university in Educom (education and community development) and now Law, I was broadcasting weekly radio programmes and researching information that was of use to our community. However I felt weakened, occasionally broken. The only contentment I had was the security of my family and now as I focused on making them 'happy', I simultaneously grew fearful of my inability to prepare them for a war in which the enemy had no moral code for rules of engagement. How dare I try living a normal life when I am fully aware these are not normal times? If these words feel disjointed it is because this poem was incredible hard to write and remains unfinished.
6 January 2011

HEALING

nwn

This was written whilst in Africa. Nwn is a Kmt term that refers to a divine mass of 'water' which all that is alive in creation is believed to emanate from. I regard water with much reverence and recognise it as a sacred catalyst for developing my own creative and personal growth. Late 2008, I travelled to Senegal in order to heal from a year of relentless physical and spiritual attacks. My energy was low, my distrust and fear of betrayal by Africans outside my immediate family was high, in short, I was almost broken.

Once I arrived in Dakar, I was almost immediately greeted by elders and healers who helped nurture my spirit back to health. Eventually I left the city to live alone in a tiny solar powered house residing in a small seaside village. Within days my strength started to return as it became clear I was at home in an area that was still infused with African tradition and ritual. There surrounded by the peace and tranquillity of nature, the majestic beauty of the warm sun and calm sea, I was able to bask in the beauty of the Creator, meditate and with help, reconnect with our Ancestors.

Following this, I wrote my book *Ukweli* and this poem. I can never quite express in words the gratitude I have for Maame Ama Gueye and family for extending me such warmth and hospitality, nor can I put a price on the wise counsel of Ayi Kwei-Armah and the Per Ankh collective whose generosity and wisdom restored my faith in the huge intellectual and socio-political capacity as well as the undeniable spiritual potential of African people to accomplish anything we consciously desire.

the cliff
Just like that first kiss, the natural high from loving an African woman is unlike anything I have ever experienced. drugs, alcohol and artificial chemical highs cannot compare.
14 November 2003

the right story
Written in response to a short but deep spiritual conversation with a friend outside Happy People restaurant following the event Love Inspires.
14 August 2008

love we
Written as a performance piece with call back and response to the audience.
25 November 2003

I remember...
The natural high from befriending a conscious African woman is addictive whilst dangerously intoxicating.

chat
The best oral sex is the natural vibe during no hold bars honest Africentric conversation.
15 November 2003

talk
Women and men are equal but different.

eating peanuts
Sometimes being hypersensitive in relationships built on an almost perfect spiritual love can lead to the flimsiest of reasons leading to major arguments that are way out of proportion of the original issue. The reality of desiring perfect physicality is that it must always come at a cost.
14 December 2003

African woman
Inspired by an article in the Guardian newspaper where the author publicly explained without apology why she could only love an African man. I realised that there is a dearth of poetry in the public domain that extol the same truth that many African men have for African women. I decided to dedicate this poem in support for Pan African women's day when I realised how rare it is to hear public affirmation of the majestic divinity of African woman from the African man. This is my contribution. Without her, I cannot be. Interestingly I received several vicious attacks by African men and european women in response.
3 August 2004

change
As those involved in relationships evolve and grow, it is essential that communication and indeed, trust is maintained. Not for us to remain the same, but for us to avoid blame by instead both willing choosing to remain.

inspire/desire
Inspired by a good friend who helped me through a traumatic time in my life. Sometimes we can be selfish to the needs of those who support us and fail to see the pain we inflict by extensively leaning on them.
November 2008 - 2009

mind over fear
Mastery of self requires discipline of self, but this does not mean restricting spirit, more obeying it.
15 August 2008

departure
On leaving a good sistah friend in the Caribbean.
5 August 2010

N'factor
I am blessed with wonderful family and friends. This was inspired by one of them who selflessly gave me support despite facing challenges I was unaware of.
1 November 2008

she saved me
Inspired by the love for my wife, Oleander.

lil'mzstuch / light / 'fro
Portraits and thoughts after meditation in
Ghana. Lil'mzstuch also reflects my feelings
after meeting my wife at a community
meeting.
22 June 2009

my man
the love of lone mothers raising our sons
without fathers often blurs the nature of the
relationship.

purple
Purple is said to be a colour that represents
spirituality and creativity, passion and
sensitivity, a combination of hot red and
cool blue. This poem was inspired following
a warm and sensitive meeting I had with a
beautiful friend as we talked, laughed and
shared space whilst it snowed on one cold
afternoon in London. A true muse.
17 December 2010.

you
In memory of my son whose spirit briefly
visited this realm.

RANDOM

Information
We live in a so called knowledge economy
where information is attached to a price. Yet
everything is information and information
is everything.
27 May 2003

free poetry
A talented young poetess named Emma relit
my interest in short creative writing
following a discussion which concluded - art
is life and all life should be free.
21 October 2002

maths
wrong
a =1, e =2, ae=1

right
a=1, e =1, aa =3

free thought
If this normal world of injustice and
inequality is not insane, then where is the
abnormal justice and equality for the sane.

nice poem (4 ken + chinua)
In the first three months of the 2001, oil
giant BP enjoyed profits of £2.86bn, the US
company Exxon Mobil reaped £3.49bn,
while the Anglo-Dutch giant Shell netted
£2.69bn. Exxon Mobil announced that it
had made a record £13.4bn profit in 2004.
Whilst ChevronTexaco recently said its
fourth quarter profits had nearly doubled to
$3.44bn, against the same period in 2003.
However in 2005 BP announced profits of
£8.7bn, a 26% rise from 2004's figures
whilst shell announced record profits for a
UK company of £9.3bn - the equivalent to
more than £1million an hour.

In the same week as the perverse February
2005 profit announcements at least two
protesters were killed after hundreds of men
and women stormed an oil installation
operated by the Nigerian arm of us giant
chevron Texaco in Nigeria's impoverished
southern delta region. The protesters from
the Ugborodo and Arutan communities
took action after the oil company failed to
deliver on earlier pledges which included
the responsibility to provide water,
electricity, schools, clinics, jobs and
development projects for neighbouring
villages.

This pledge was made after 600 village
women took over ChevronTexaco's *Escravos*
terminal in 2002. At the time
ChevronTexaco officials said some of the
women's 23 demands would take time to
fulfil, while others - such as a demand to
build 80,000 houses - were unrealistic.
ChevronTexaco representative Dick Filgate
declared at one point. "I've put everything
on the table that I am prepared to give... I
want *Escravos* back. I want the ladies off the
site." but after the American oil executive
pounded his fist on the table he was
interrupted by a representative of the village
chief who warned him "in our culture, only
the chief pounds the table".

Filgate, general manager of asset
management for ChevronTexaco's *Nigeria*
subsidiary concluded "I can't give you

everything on the list but I am prepared to continue the dialogue". The women were disappointed the company had not firmly agreed to hire village men.

The historic struggle between international oil firms and local communities drew international attention in the mid-1990s, when protests by the tiny *Ogoni* tribe turned violent and forced shell to abandon its wells on their land. As a response, in 1995 the late dictator general Sane Abacha responded by hanging nine *Ogoni* leaders, including noted writer *Ken Saro Wiwa*. This triggered international outrage which led to *Nigeria's* expulsion from the British commonwealth.

This poem was written in honour of the political activist *Kenule Beeson Saro-Wiwa* who promoted issues such as this and the western bias against African languages and literature .

"the writer cannot be a mere storyteller; he cannot be a mere teacher; he cannot merely X-ray society's weaknesses, its ills, its perils. He or she must be actively involved in shaping its present and its future."
Ken Saro-Wiwa (1941-1995).

silence
Written whilst in Africa after observing the vulnerability of some women to predatory men

URBANODITY

black anthem
Dr. John Henrik Clarke famously said that powerful people will never educate powerless people in how to take away their power. He also reminded us to never forget that that being mechanised was not the same as being civilised.

politics of hair
The afro is a natural African hairstyle not a sub 'urban' ethnicity. The desire to make our hair unnatural is a curse alongside that of skin whitening, both men and women must address.
10 December 2004

home
Western media produces self hating ideological propaganda to support weak confused African men too frightened (or stupid) to accept the Truth that their natural home is with the African woman.

1 2 3
Inspired by the new generation of "we" poets who performed at Nylon
8 December 2003

broken word
As the spoken word movement grows in strength and popularity there has been numerous attempts to urbanise it into a commercial product thereby depoliticising it in a similar manner as was done to hip hop

that song/bLack and urban
Too many African performers pimp out our culture for awards that denigrate our women, identity and spiritual integrity by promoting usage of offensive images and labels such as the n word and 'mf. Sadly they are endorsed by award organisation such as MOBO which once sought to change its identity from the music of 'black' origin to music of 'urban' origin. The true moniker should be music of 'bloodied' origin.

behind
In response to the bbc launching a controversial and disrespectful poster of 4 naked brothas in the shower as part of its campaign for its babyfather drama. The billboard was displayed across London.
November 2002

right on white
Seeking publicity and controversy Peter Tatchell of Outrage claims on choice fm radio debate show that Malcolm X and most of our great (African) leaders were either 'gay' or bisexual.
6 December 2003

backing black
Written about political illiteracy – After reading Chuck D of Public Enemy, one of my childhood hip-hop heroes claim he is backing Obama because he is 'black'
1 November 2008

AWAKENING

If
15 March 2005

the day the lie died
My last ever electoral vote was for the UK's Labour party, a mistake I did not replicate. I will now never endorse a political party that does not explicitly commit to addressing our concerns.

an uncivil war
Inspired by debate on Misogyny after an online discussion descended into a fracas where African men attacked both African women and men for fighting sexism.
December 2005

25 in 24
The 2004 tsunami is renamed the Asian tsunami and touches the heart of the 'international' community as the world reveals its contempt for Africa.

Perhaps if the uber-trendy, morally dishonest *Make Poverty History* campaign had been renamed Make Capitalism History from the onset then meaningful political change could have occurred. Perhaps.

aid
of the 42 million people infected with HIV, 28 million are in Africa.
July 2003.

state revenge
A review of the terrorist laws rushed through parliament after September 11th revealed that they required the UK to opt out of the human rights agreement it had signed up to. Surprisingly the new laws weren't deemed racist despite the fact they only targeted 'foreign' nationals.
18 December

democrazy falls
In response to president bush and prime minister Tony Blair's claims of wanting to spread us style democracy all over the world.
4 October 2004

paedo files?
Less than three months after the government reveals plans to create a comprehensive, intrusive and immoral database on all children in the UK, the home secretary reveals that the government will launch an inquiry into investigating how police vetting procedures failed and murderer Ian Huntley was allowed to work with children despite past allegations of rape and accusations of underage sex.

In interviews after his conviction the police justify the 'weeding' of these historical files citing compliance with the data protection act. the following morning the media reveal details of operation (s)Pin, a 'new' police initiative to crack down on people who surf the internet looking for child abuse (pornographic) pictures. the question whether these same data protection laws will apply to the child 'protection' database remains unasked?

Note: Since this poem was written, the catholic church has been exposed as having actively covering up thousands of child abuse cases protecting thousands of the perverted members of the clergy within its body.
17 December 2003

the racists are gone
Invoked by a discussion with Emma on the efforts British society makes to hide its racist nature.

truth holes
First thoughts on hearing of the 'capture' of Saddam Hussein in a hole.
14 December 2003

hate crimes more likely
Statistics reveal 'black' men are eight times more likely to be stopped and searched than any other racial group in London.
November 2002

Words most used (In order of frequency)
African, Love, Free, Life, Words, Truth

List of Images

Speaking Truth to Power by Tajudeen Abdul-Raheem
Community support outside the court trial of Toyin Agbetu
Octavia Butler
Fighting the Slave Trade edited by Sylviane A Diouf
Two Thousand Seasons by Ayi Kwei Armah
General History of Africa published by UNESCO
The African origin of Civilisation by Cheikh Anta Diop
African Philosophy (The Pharonic Period: 2780-330 BC) by Theophile Obenga
Sankofa by Haile Gerima
Muhammad Ali
United Friends and Families demonstration
Toyin Agbetu at Westminster Abbey, 27 March 2007
African World Revolution by John Henrik Clarke
Miriam Makeba and her husband Kwame Ture
African Voices by Ms Serwah and Kwaku
Rosa Parkes
Claudia Jones
Frank Crichlow (front, far right)
Notting Hill carnival remembrance flyer (3 mins silence) and police penalty notice
Corrupt police officers in Nigeria
Fela Kuti and Afrika 70's Zombie album
The Spirit of Intimacy by Sobonfu Somé
Myth, Literature and the African World by Wole Soyinka
Extension of a Man by Donny Hathaway
The Phoenix – Misrule in the land of Nod by Onyeka Nubia
Police cower behind shields during Brixton uprising, 1981
Ogun beads
Butterfly
The Healers by Ayi Kwei-Armah
Afropick logo
Forever Young, Gifted and Black by Nina Simone
Swan
Kola Nut
Gods Bits of Wood by Ousmane Sembène
Seasons Change by Fertile Ground
Mbuya Nehanda
Winnie and Nelson Mandela with daughter Zindzi
Elephants ritualise around the bones of their Ancestors in remembrance
The Bussa memorial statue in Barbados
Me and my sister Funmi Womack
The Miseducation of Lauryn Hill
An Oleander
A young, female, black panther
Acoustic soul by India Arie
African sunset
Nyansapo, an Adinkra symbol for wisdom
Bernie Grant, the first true Pan Africanist MP in British parliament, 1996
Hariet Tubman
Ken Saro-Wiwa

Half of a Yellow Sun by Chimamanda Ngozi Adichie
Cowrie shells
Rain on a skylight
A Cylon from Battlestar Galactica
Beautifully Human by Jill Scott
MOBO – A Music of Bloodied Origins award for promotion of the n word, bitch and 'mf' epithets
BBC street poster campaign for its *Babyfather* TV series
The Voice news publication logo
The MOBO logo sponsored by Western Union
Malcolm X
Barack Obama
Public Enemy
Martin Luther King
Equal Rights by Peter Tosh
Thomas Sankara Speaks
The Destruction of Black Civilisation by Chancellor Williams
Make Poverty History campaigners
Obedient boy of empire trinket given to those formally joining the ranks of Officer of the Order of the British Empire
Over 180 innocent African children detained, searched and held in custody by police force officers armed with machine guns, 25 August 2008.

Note: If there are any errors or information missing from this list please contact us with the correct details.

Also available:

Ukweli – A Political and spiritual basis for Pan Africanism

"Freedom and dignity through the work of liberation"

Pan Africanism only works when politics and spirituality is at the heart of its teachings. Its ethos of education and community development only occurs when the spiritual essence is peacemaking and the most political expression is that of progressive community building.

In this intimate book of instruction, Toyin Agbetu explains why Pan Africanism is still relevant in today's world. He explains how knowledge of our ancient history and wisdoms has helped win battles in a war of enslavement that begun hundreds of years ago. If you've ever wondered about your purpose and responsibility to community, or question whether rites of passage would help our children, then come follow his journey and read his words of learning in this merging of spirit and politics.

Ukweli is the Kiswahili word for Truth

Publisher   Ligali
Published   13 April 2010
ISBN-13   978-0-9543443-6-8

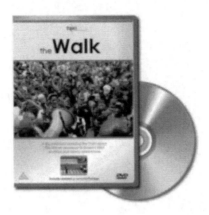

The Walk - DVD

On 27 March 2007 a Pan Africanist named Toyin Agbetu challenged the British Government, Monarchy and Church as they gathered to hold a religious celebration for the Bicentenary of the Abolition of the Slave Trade Act in Westminster Abbey, England. The ritual, which made no mention of the Haitian Revolution, the Middle Passage and the African freedom fighters that ended Britain's system of transatlantic and colonial enslavement focused on the acts of parliamentarian William Wilberforce.

Toyin, who condemned the service as an insult and disgrace, halted the proceedings with words that gave a voice to the collective view of millions around the world. As Maafa truths were revealed he was demonised and misrepresented in the British media as a 'lone madman'.

Watch the restored uncensored footage of what happened that day and afterwards when the African community in Britain stood beside him - from his arrest and incarceration to the eventual dropping of all criminal charges. Their journey took them from Westminster Abbey, outside Downing Street, the National Portrait Gallery, Africa House and eventually to the belongings of their Ancestors still illegally held captive in the British Museum.

This is the story of their walk...

Directed by Toyin Agbetu / Produced by emma pierre

Feature Running Time: 121 minutes approx
Main Soundtrack: English Stereo
Video Aspect Ratio: 16:9 (Widescreen)